The Social Work Pocket Guide to… Direct Obse

By Siobhan Maclean and Mick Baker

First Edition 2013 ISBN: 978-1-903575-87-1

A catalogue record for this book will be availab̲

©Kirwin Maclean Associates Ltd 4 Mesnes Green, Lichfield, Staffs, WS14 9AB

Contents List...

What?

Why?

How?

WHAT?

'You can observe a lot by watching' (Berra 2008). This quote from the American baseball player in the 60's in response to a reporter's question, sums up the process very well. There is of course more to it than that, but in essence he is correct; observation is pretty much about watching.

Watching is essentially a natural human activity that requires little thought or analysis. However, for the process of directly observing others in the context of social work education this 'natural activity' needs to be carefully considered.

This section will explore the following questions:

- What is direct observation?
- What do we mean by observer / observee?
- What are the origins of the approach?
- What are the main models of direct observation?
- What is the Hawthorne effect?

WHAT IS DIRECT OBSERVATION ALL ABOUT?

Direct Observation is...

...rather like breathing: life depends on it and we do it all the time, usually without reflection. (Peberdy 1993)

...part of the process of looking, seeing and understanding reality. Observation is also a universal activity which is continuous and characterised by passivity and lack of involvement. (Le Riche 1998)

...the most obvious form of assessment for practical, skills-based subjects. It is therefore the recommended default form of assessment for competency-based programmes. (Atherton 2011)

What?

...an active experience for everyone involved. It is a practice which continues to offer rewards as long as you pursue it. (Lloyd Webber 2010)

...the most straightforward of all assessment techniques because it involves just what it implies: the direct observation and recording of... behaviours in the context in which they occur. (Spielberger 2004)

...watching people and recording their behaviour on the spot. (Bernard 2006)

...a non-intrusive research method, seen as having high face validity - also referred to as external validity or ecological validity. (Hu 2011)

The observer and observee

Throughout this Guide we have referred to the observer and observee. To clarify, we have used these words in the following way:

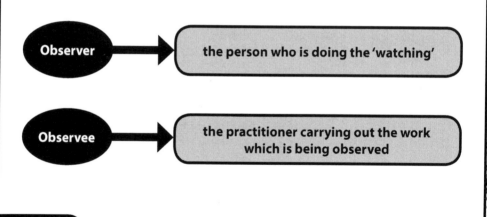

Observer → the person who is doing the 'watching'

Observee → the practitioner carrying out the work which is being observed

What?

The observer might be a practice educator or on-site supervisor carrying out an observation of a student's practice. Increasingly, social work managers are carrying out direct observations of team members - particularly of newly qualified workers (NQSWs).

The practice of peer observation (one practitioner observing another) is growing in popularity in social work - particularly with the implementation of the Assessed and Supported Year in Employment (ASYE) and the Professional Capabilities Framework (PCF) in England. So increasingly anyone can be an observer or an observee.

The origins of direct observation

The origins of direct observation lie in research, where direct observation is a method used within qualitative research.

Quantative research gathers data in numerical form, whereas qualitative research gathers more descriptive data. Qualitative research is commonly used in the social sciences where the researcher seeks to understand the 'how and why' of aspects of human behaviour rather than simply the 'what'.

Qualitative approaches to research draw on a variety of methods, including participant observation and direct observation.

What?

Participant Observation

This requires the researcher to become an active participant in the activity or culture being observed. This method usually requires weeks or months in order for the researcher to be accepted as part of the culture, enabling accurate findings to emerge.

Direct Observation

This differs from participant observation in that the researcher is not part of the event taking place. The researcher is able to adopt a detached view of the event although this in itself can potentially impact on the findings of such research as the researcher is likely to influence the interaction being observed.

13

Types of Direct Observation

It is generally accepted that there are two types of direct observation:

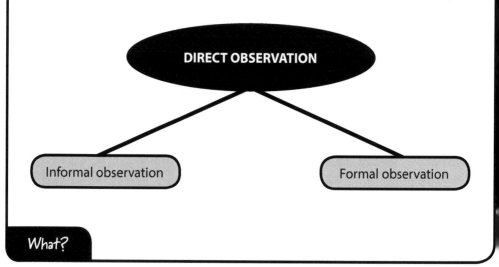

DIRECT OBSERVATION

Informal observation

Formal observation

Informal Observation

In research methodology, informal observation is referred to as 'free' or unstructured observation. Informal observations are basically observations of events or behaviour which are unplanned and unstructured.

Informal observations of practice are often used in social work. For example, students on placement are being observed all the time - during their interaction with other members of the team, in team meetings or simply in the office environment on a day-to-day basis. This informal observation will perhaps consider the student's interpersonal skills, whether they are respectful to others or whether they communicate effectively by telephone. The process of observation is therefore ongoing and will (perhaps unconsciously) contribute to the final assessment of the student.

Formal Observation

Planned direct observations of practice have been a requirement in social work education and training for some time, and the use of formal observations in ensuring good practice in social work generally is increasing. Although informal observation occurs on an ongoing basis, formal observation will include a planning stage and should result in formal feedback.

Formal observations of practice are generally used to inform an assessment of capability in social work practice. As such, the use of formal observations in social work is similar to the use of formal observation as a research method. The observer is essentially 'researching' the quality of practice being observed.

Based on their work with trainee teachers, Weade and Evertson (1991) identified an 'observation continuum'. They contrast everyday informal observation that occurs subconsciously with formal observation which is used for the purpose of assessment. The data collected from the informal

What?

observation will be absorbed but not necessarily used formally in the assessment process. Weade and Evertson conclude that the process of observation does not just move through a continuum but provides a *'feedback loop with information from the formal and informal observations interacting together to inform the picture of the world around us'* (Le Riche 1998). The evidence generated from both formal and informal observations of practice will therefore combine to provide a picture of the practitioner's level of work.

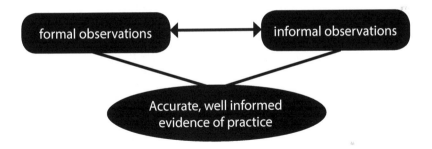

Retrospective Observation

Retrospective observation is a particular form of informal observation that is worth specific mention. An aspect of practice may be informally observed and could be drawn on later as evidence of a particular area of practice. Often retrospective observation evidence is utilised when practice educators and students are reviewing the standards they need to have addressed. They may at this stage identify a piece of practice which was observed in some way, by either the practice educator or another practitioner. The event may not have been identified as one to be observed formally, but may have generated sufficient evidence to be used as a contribution to the assessment of the student's competence. The use of retrospective observation must be viewed with caution in relation to any assessment of practice, since it is unlikely that an event which went badly would be considered. There is therefore the danger that evidence gained from retrospective observations would not necessarily constitute a true reflection of the student's practice over the course of the placement.

What?

Models of Observation

Le Riche and Tanner (1996) identified three main models of observation in social work education:

Scientific model

This model focuses on the reliability, validity and accuracy of the data. It is an objective approach requiring accurate mathematical measurement. In this model, researchers record and understand specific behaviour which is thought to be problematic. The model originated from the natural sciences where knowledge gained from laboratory experiments began to influence understanding in a range of other disciplines.

Narrative model

This approach lends itself more to the direct observation of social work practice and education. It focuses on the interpretation of information gathered by the observer. It is subjective and is based on what the observer thinks and feels about what they see. The observer makes use of their feelings and thoughts. The observer takes account of the context of the event as well as environmental factors that may impact on the observation. The observation is recorded in a written report. It is recognised that this report is based on a reconstruction of the observer's recollection of the event and their interpretation of it.

What?

Equality model

This model includes some of the elements of the previous two but addresses issues of power and authority inherent within the process of observation. Le Riche and Tanner (1996) highlight three stages to this model:

1. Negotiation is paramount in the initial stages. Careful planning around practicalities is required. There will also need to be discussion about the status of the observer and what their role and responsibilities are.

2. This model emphasises the importance of reflection and that prior to the observation it is made clear that sufficient time will be allowed for the observer to reflect on the observation.

3. The recording of the observation and who will share the findings is also discussed. Consideration should be given as to who should have access to the report.

Collaborative Model

This model was developed by the University of York in 2000. Using Le Riche and Tanner's typology (1996) it would be seen as an example of an equality model. It focuses on a collaborative approach, whereby the student takes a lead role in the setting of goals, objectives and future learning. It is described as an empowering approach which encourages close and meaningful partnership between the student and their assessor.

The model divides the direct observation into three stages:

 Before the observation, the student and the observer meet together to plan the observation, during which time they negotiate and agree:

- a set of assessment objectives. The model suggests that the observer and the student identify 2/3 objectives each.

- what they want to get/give feedback on. These can be areas that need development or where the student needs affirmation of good practice.

What?

The observation takes place with the assessor focussing on the objectives agreed in the planning stage.

After the observation the student and observer meet together to discuss how it went. The feedback remains focussed on the objectives which were agreed at Stage 1.

- The student is invited to give their evaluation first - they identify what went well, not so well and what they have learned.

- The assessor follows, giving their evaluation.

- The feedback session is concluded with a reflective discussion, based around four areas:
  - surprises
  - satisfactions
  - dissatisfactions
  - learning

23

Tavistock Model (Child observation)

The use of direct observation in social work training has links to the Tavistock model of child and infant observation devised by Esther Bick (1964). The Tavistock model has informed other research into the use of observation in social work education, reflective practice and practice assessment (Trowell and Miles 1991).

The Tavistock model recognises that direct observation basically adopts a 'fly on the wall' approach which will have an impact on the dynamics of the event being observed. This approach differs to that of participant observation where the observer is 'mentally and emotionally engaged' in the event being observed, enabling the observer to give meaning to their experience (Tanner 1998).

The Tavistock model generally involves the observer engaging in a regular series of observed events to enable the observer to generate sufficient information from which to draw conclusive findings. The observer does not

What?

take notes during the observed event as the model recognises that this could detract from the observation. Instead, the observer records their findings after the event, which is felt to enable a more objective summary of their feelings following the observation.

The model concludes with a structured opportunity for reflection. This involves small seminar groups enabling the observer time to reflect on their experiences in an environment where it is safe for them to express their feelings and anxieties, obtaining feedback on their conclusions.

Hawthorne Effect

Practitioners should always be mindful of the
'Hawthorne Effect' (Rothlisberger and Dickson 1939)
when observing practice. This term was coined
following a study carried out in the 1930s at the
Hawthorne Works, an electrical engineering company
near Chicago. The study attempted to assess whether
workers productivity was influenced by light levels in
the workplace. A number of years later, researchers
recognised that the data generated from the study
suggested that productivity increased while the
research was being carried out and slumped when
it had been concluded. The conclusion being that
individuals modify their behaviour simply as a reaction to being observed.
This suggests that overt observation cannot always be relied upon to provide
accurate evidence of performance.

What?

The Hawthorne Effect highlights the potential benefits to researchers of a covert approach to observation which may limit the impact of being observed providing a more realistic version of events. Whilst covert observations are not ethical in relation to direct observations in social work, where a practitioner is used to their observer being around in the workplace, informal observation can limit the impact of the Hawthorne Effect.

For the 'visible observer' (Wilson and Corlett 2005) the Hawthorne Effect clearly presents a challenge around how to minimise the impact of the observer's participation in the events being observed. Careful planning of the observation and triangulating the evidence generated, will all help to limit the impact of the Hawthorne Effect. Guidance on the most effective methods to employ when directly observing practice is included in the 'How?' section of this Guide.

We began this section by stating that direct observation is essentially about watching.

When people are asked to carry out an observation of someone else's practice, they often lack confidence and are not sure what to do. Maybe that's because watching is an activity which we generally take for granted.

This section provides the basis for understanding how to undertake observations of practice.

What?

WHY?

Direct observations are a standard requirement of most social work training programmes at both qualifying and post qualifying levels; however, this is not the only reason why observations of practice should take place in social work practice. This section considers the following questions:

- Why are direct observations of practice so important in social work?
- Why do people become anxious about direct observations?

In exploring the importance of direct observations, this section considers the benefits of direct observation for the four key stakeholders.

WHY IS DIRECT OBSERVATION SO IMPORTANT IN SOCIAL WORK?

Requirements for direct observations of practice

Requirements for direct observations of practice in social work education and training are relatively new.

Indeed, according to Danbury (1994: 100) in the fairly recent past, *"direct observation was not considered to be viable, as it was a firmly held belief that the relationship between student and client would be damaged, possibly irreparably".*

The use of direct observation was formally introduced to social work training in the Diploma in Social Work through 'Paper 30' in 1991. At a similar time, requirements for practice teachers to be observed as part of their assessment was introduced.

It seems impossible now that professional practice could ever have been assessed without practice being directly observed as a key part of that assessment.

Why?

The importance of direct observation in assessing social work practice was soon recognised at all levels of practice and is now used in social work education and training at all levels.

With the implementation of the Professional Capabilities Framework (PCF) in England, social work is moving towards the holistic assessment of competence (or capability). Holistic assessment draws on direct observation as a rich source of evidence and it is likely therefore that direct observations of social work practice will become even more regular in the future.

According to Skills for Care (2013 online) the emphasis on the ongoing assessment of even the most experienced workers means that the process of directly observing practice will continue to be a key feature of social work education and continuous professional development.

Benefits of direct observation

There are many benefits to direct observation. So much so that where direct observations have been required as part of qualification programmes, candidates have made an active decision to continue with occasional observations even after the qualification has been completed.

The benefits of direct observations can be viewed in terms of four key 'players':

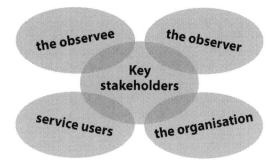

Why?

The Observer

For observers, direct observation can:

- provide first hand evidence of the observee's practice
- enable them to provide more meaningful and evidenced feedback which can support the practitioner to develop their practice
- highlight aspects of the practitioner's practice which fall below required standards
- identify the challenges to best practice
- enable them to develop their own observational skills
- provide a significant learning opportunity. The observer may see aspects of practice they have not experienced themselves and they can certainly learn from watching another's practice

The Observee

There are a range of benefits to direct observations for the person being observed. For example, direct observation:

- provides the opportunity to receive a different perspective on their work
- enables them to develop reflection on their practice, drawing on evidenced feedback
- provides an opportunity to demonstrate capability and receive confirmation of their abilities
- allows them to develop their own observational skills which are essential for good social work practice
- identifies areas of difficulty and allows them to receive support and guidance to facilitate learning

Why?

- has the potential to be empowering - enabling the observee to take greater control of their practice
- can increase confidence in their own abilities and in being observed
- acts as an active CPD activity. A well planned and structured observation will provide a range of learning for the practitioner being observed

Despite the fact that being observed provokes anxiety, it is well worth arranging for your practice to be observed

The Service User

There are a number of benefits to good quality person-centred direct observations. For service users, direct observations can:

- act as a safeguard for good practice - since the work of the practitioner is open to scrutiny from a more experienced professional

- improve the service they receive

- create a meaningful opportunity to evaluate the service received

- recognise the expertise of the service user and their lived experience

- promote confidence through involvement in social work education and training and service improvement

Why?

It is important to be aware that these benefits for service users will only occur where observations are carried out well. Poor practice in observations (for example, not seeking consent, not drawing on feedback etc) will mean that the service user can have negative experiences in the observation and may well feel disempowered.

The main thing to remember is that all social work practice should be focussed on the needs and views of service users and this focus must extend into social work education, training and professional development. The involvement of service users and carers in social work education and training must be more than tokenistic. Unfortunately, whilst progress has been made, many service users feel that 'lip-service' is still paid to service user and carer participation in social work education (Branfield 2007).

The Organisation

The observer, observee and service user will be present in a direct observation of practice, so they are always recognised as key stakeholders. However, the importance of direct observations of practice to the organisation are often missed. Recognising the value of observations of practice, many social work employers have made direct observations a requirement (often arranged as part of the supervisory process). The benefits of direct observations to the organisation include:

- observations can highlight both tensions and opportunities in relation to the application of policy and procedure in practice
- service users can provide feedback on the effectiveness of the service provided, promoting participation and co-production
- where observations are carried out regularly, practice is likely to improve

Why?

- the process of direct observations should promote reflection and learning in the organisation - which will impact on the culture of the organisation creating a more critically reflective organisation

- observations can provide evidence for the measurement of outcomes and can therefore provide a clearer organisational evidence base

The learning that can be achieved through service user and carer involvement in assessment is not just important for the development of individuals but also for the development of a culture in which whole organisations 'learn' to understand and be more responsive to the needs and wishes of its service users.

(Williams and Rutter 2007: 121)

Why are people anxious about direct observations?

Think about a time when you have been observed in practice or talk to anyone about their experiences of being observed, and one of the first things that comes up is how nervous people are about being observed.

Being observed can be anxiety provoking for a range of reasons:

- being watched gives a feeling of being "under the microscope". In itself, this creates anxiety

- very often the observee has a significant 'investment' in the observation. The observation is generally linked to a qualification or at least an assessment of capability

> **I was so nervous about my practice educator coming with me that I almost crashed my car on the way.**

Why?

- leading on from this 'investment' and from the fact that the observer is generally in a supervisory position over the observee, there are significant power dynamics in the observation process. The observee may well feel powerless in the situation

Observations will always create 'nerves' but observers should work in partnership with the observee to limit any anxiety. The University of York (2000) note that whilst anxiety impedes learning, a state of apprehension leaves people open to learning. It is therefore vital that the reasons people feel anxious about being observed are acknowledged by the observer. Discussing these issues and how they can be handled is the main way in which a person who is being observed can move from a state of anxiety to apprehension.

> **It just felt so false that I worried about it for a good week or so. I hardly slept the night before the observation.**

41

Power dynamics

The relationship between an observee and observer is influenced by the power dynamics inherent within the roles each perform during the observation. As a key player in the observation process, the service user also has power in the situation.

The impact of power can be subtle at times, involving wider forces and influences which are generated outside and beyond the event being observed.

To understand the power dynamics in direct observations, it is important to recognise the various sources of power at play.

Why?

Sources of power

In a 1959 study which is now seen as a classic, French and Raven identified five sources or types of power:

Legitimate or positional power: This is power that exists because of the way an organisation is structured or through how society is ordered. People have power because of their position within an organisation - for example, an observer is likely to be in a more senior position in an organisation.

Expert or professional power: This is where a person is seen as having a particular bank of knowledge or expertise. Observers generally hold expert power based on their professional training, qualification and experience.

Reward power: This is power gained through the ability to give 'rewards' of some kind. In social work, those who assess and make plans can hold a significant amount of reward power, for example in making decisions about eligibility and what services can be offered to people.

Referent power: This is power created by the admiration and respect a person can have for another person. This can be based on individual characteristics (or charisma) or it can be based on admiration that people have for people from a particular profession. A good example of this is a person's respect for their GP (although the GP's power is also derived from legitimate and expert power). Observers may hold referent power if the observee admires and respects the observer's practice.

Coercive power: This is power based on the ability to apply punishment or sanctions. This power is most keenly felt in children's services (going to court for a care order) and mental health services (around the use of the Mental Health Act). The service user could be conscious of this power even if it has not been actively applied by social workers. Coercive power can be seen as the most obvious form of power and it is perhaps the form of power which is most likely to build resentment or defensiveness from people on the receiving end of it.

Why?

The Inner London Probation Service (1993) recognised French and Raven's sources of power, but added two additional sources of power:

Societal power: This is the power based on the ideology of superiority. It illustrates what we know about oppression and social exclusion. People from devalued groups experience oppression at the hands of members of more valued groups. Oppressors are powerful and oppressed people are less powerful. For example, a woman who experiences sexism will feel less powerful than a man.

The power to determine: The Inner London Probation Service examines the power dynamics in practice education and refer to this power as the power a practice educator has to 'pass or fail' a student. In many ways the power to determine, is simply the power to make decisions which determine outcomes for another person. Social workers can have the power to determine in a number of ways – for example in making decisions about action to be taken.

Understanding sources of power is vitally important in carrying out observations of practice. Indeed, in preparing for an observation, it can be useful to explore the sources of power, considering each of the participants in the observation. Carrying out an exercise reflecting on the sources of power and the potential impact of these before an observation, then returning to this and considering how power may have impacted on the observation after the process, can provide an excellent learning opportunity for everyone involved. The power dynamics in a direct observation will differ significantly based on who is involved in the practice being observed, but some reflections might include:

Service users have influence over the dynamic of the observation. For example the service user may prefer to converse with who they perceive to hold the power, which is likely to be the observer. They may think that the observer is 'the expert' and they may feel that it is in their best interest to engage with the observer as opposed to the person being observed.

The service user may also hold 'expert power' as they have influence regarding the feedback process and this may be viewed as an empowering process for many service users.

Why?

Observee. The observee's power is derived from their role within the interaction with the service user. They have the power to make decisions regarding the service user's assessment and service provision. They may also carry with them societal power associated with belonging to a powerful group.

Observer. The observer's power is perhaps the most obvious. They will have the responsibility to judge whether the person being observed has achieved the required standard and advise on any future development. As Humphrey (2008) states, practice educators *"are expert practitioners as a result of their training and experience, and they have been endowed with legitimate authority over students by their agency and university."*

Although each participant has the potential to exert power during the observation, it is clear that the observer has the most power in terms of their influence over the outcome. As Tsui (2005) highlights *"the use of authority and power is not usually welcomed by frontline social workers who value care, equality, teamwork and staff participation."* The observer therefore, needs to reflect on how power will manifest itself in the event being observed and what strategies can be used to redress this imbalance.

In considering aspects of power, it can be easy to 'miss' key issues around diversity. However, issues around diversity and societal power will have a significant influence on the situation. For example, in discussing this issue we reflected on our personal experiences. Mick, as a man, often finds that service users look to him and refer questions to him - trying to engage him in the social work process. As a woman, I have found that this happens less often and occasionally, despite explanations, service users have sometimes assumed that I am 'learning the job' - especially when I am observing mature male students.

It is important, therefore, to reflect on aspects of identity and diversity in preparing for any direct observation of practice.

> **The dynamics of power inherent in relationships involving difference, whether it be of race, culture, age, gender or physical ability will be experienced in observation.**
> (Le Riche and Tanner, 1996)

Why?

HOW?

Despite the known importance of direct observations of practice, those responsible for carrying out observations often report feeling anxious and ill-prepared. This section provides guidance on best practice in direct observation in order to ensure that:

- observations are user-centred and focussed
- the potential for direct observation in terms of both learning and assessment is maximised

HOW DO I GET THE MOST OUT OF DIRECT OBSERVATIONS?

Guidelines for best practice

To ensure best practice in direct observation, an observer can put a range of measures in place. These include the observer:

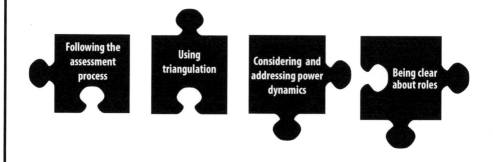

- Following the assessment process
- Using triangulation
- Considering and addressing power dynamics
- Being clear about roles

How?

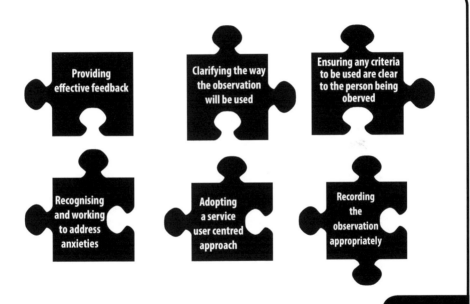

51

Following the Assessment Process

Any assessment process has four distinct stages, forming a cycle of assessment as follows:

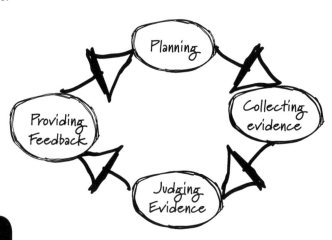

Since direct observation is a method of assessment, the assessment process can be applied, as follows:

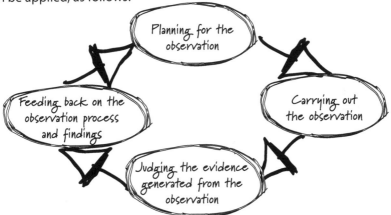

This section begins by exploring each of these four stages of the observation process.

Planning for the Observation

Reflecting the fact that observations of practice should be user-centred and that the service user's needs always take priority over those of the observee and observer, thoughts around planning the observation should begin with a consideration of the service user's needs.

Planning around the service user's needs

In preparing for the observation the permission of the service user must be sought. This is particularly important, as the needs of the service user should always be paramount. Discussion with family and / or carers may also take place to ensure that all the relevant parties agree to the event being observed. Tanner (1998) highlights the importance of considering the needs of the service user in relation to consent. *"Careful consideration must be given to issues such as cognitive ability, language capacity, developmental stage, and the process of negotiation adapted to meet the needs of the individual. The views should also be*

How?

sought of a child's parents, or carers significant in the life of a vulnerable adult, as to when and how the negotiation will take place and who it would be helpful to involve."

Consideration should be given as to how the detail of the observation is to be explained to the service user. As part of the planning stage, the practitioner who is being observed will need to reflect on how the role of the observer will be explained and how the process may impact on the service user.

In our experience of direct observation the role of the observer can be confusing and ambiguous for the service user. Is the observer observing them or the student? Is the process part of the service user's assessment? Is the observation linked to the outcome for the service user in terms of resources? Why does the observer not say anything? These are issues which will need to be addressed prior to the observation, to provide some clarity to the service user and others present.

Following most direct observations, the service user will be asked to provide feedback on the observation. The observee will need to explain the process of providing feedback clearly and concisely, reducing any potential for anxiety before seeking the service user's agreement to provide feedback.

<u>Other Planning Issues</u>

Other issues that need to be covered in the planning process include:

Planning around intervention: The potential for intervention by the observer needs to be addressed in the planning stage of the observation. Kingston and Smith (1983) suggest that *"rehearsal of such factors as at what point it might be necessary to intervene, should be an essential part of the preparation."* They argue that the scenario in which it will be appropriate for the observer to intervene needs to be agreed beforehand. This will reduce the potential for any confusion during the observation and the observee will have clarity as to what to expect from the observer. It will reduce the possibility of the observee looking to the observer for guidance and advice and viewing the observer

How?

as the 'expert'. Making this clear before the observation should enable the observee to prepare effectively and to take responsibility for their practice.

Transport and arrivals: Whilst this seems straightforward, it is often one of the areas that creates most difficulty. We like to think of this as 'choreographing arrivals' as follows:

CHOREOGRAPHING ARRIVALS CAREFULLY IS IMPORTANT

- Will the observer and observee travel together?
- If they are travelling separately, where will they meet? It is preferable not to meet outside the service user's home - for a variety of reasons (they really need to arrive on the doorstep together).

The practicality of providing some immediate feedback and how the transport arrangements will impact on this also needs to be considered.

Once the parties have arrived at the event, introductions will be made. The observee and observer should agree beforehand as to who will make the introductions and who will explain how the observation will be carried out. Permission should also be sought from the service user or their representatives a final time before the observation begins.

When should this planning take place?

It is important to leave sufficient time between the preparation and the observation for any actions to be carried out. However, it's also important that the preparation doesn't take place too far ahead of the observation. We find that a week or so before the observation is a good time for the preparation discussion.

How?

Carrying out the observation

There is a great deal to consider when carrying out the observation of practice, including:

- how the observation will be recorded - both as it is occurring and afterwards
- maintaining an awareness of roles in the observation and the way that these can be dynamic
- keeping the power dynamics in mind and working to address these
- considering how best to obtain service user feedback

  These issues are covered in more detail once this section has covered the process of direct observation

- employing reflective practice techniques
- the potential sources of error in assessing the observation

MOST IMPORTANTLY OF ALL, ENSURE THAT THE SERVICE USER'S NEEDS REMAIN PARAMOUNT THROUGHOUT AND THAT THE ASSESSMENT IS PERSON-CENTRED.

Judging Evidence

Having carried out the observation, the observer needs to make an informed judgement about the quality of the practitioner's performance and ensure that the evidence informing this judgement is valid. The power of the observer at this point is clear as *"the power to define the truth"* lies with them (Cowburn, Nelson, Williams 2000).

Murrell (1993) identified two phases of making observational judgements:

Process Stage	the information received by the observer is sifted and put into categories

Inference Stage	the observer must interpret this information against their own subjective evaluation

How?

Kemshall (1993) highlights how observations are passed through a filter of typifications, past experiences, expectations, prejudices, and knowledge. The challenge for the observer is therefore to ensure that any judgement is subject to rigorous processes which will include their own evaluation. Tanner and Le Riche (1995) describe the importance of observers reflecting on the evidence they have before imposing theoretical perspectives or rushing into premature judgements.

In making a judgement about the information they have gathered during an observation, observers may find two frameworks particularly useful:

Korthagen's reflective onion

VACS criteria

61

Korthagen's Reflective Onion

Korthagen's work on reflective practice is not widely used in social work practice. The reflective onion was devised as a model to promote reflective practice for teachers and some of the language in the model demonstrates these roots. However, it can be used very effectively to promote deeper reflection in social work practice.

Korthagen's model (eg: 2005) is based on the layers of an onion. As each layer of the 'onion' is considered and peeled back to reveal the next layer, reflection on the event goes deeper.

As social workers, we know that reflective practice helps us to make sense of a situation and helps to provide more clearly evidence based judgements. This understanding can be applied to observations of social work practice where using a specific model to reflect on what has been observed can really help the observer to make an informed judgement.

How?

environment
behaviour
competences
beliefs
identity

mission

Korthagen's reflective onion refers to the 'layers' of reflection. As each layer is considered and peeled back, the reflection goes deeper.

It can be useful to draw on Korthagen's model to evaluate any direct observation of practice and make a judgement about the evidence generated. For example, the observer should reflect on:

Environment: What impact did the environment have on what I was observing? Did the practitioner draw on their observations of the environment and use these to good effect?

Behaviour: How did the practitioner behave? What were other people doing?

Competences: What skills did I observe? What competence was demonstrated?

Beliefs: How did the practitioner draw on, and apply, social work values to their practice? What impact are my values having on how I am judging the evidence generated from the observation?

Identity: What was the impact of the identity of the practitioner? How did they draw on the 'use of self' in the observation? Were there any issues of identity diversity? How did the practitioner work with these? What was the impact of my identity as observer?

How?

Mission: What were the practitioner's goals for the session? To what extent did they achieve these?

It can also be useful to ask the observee to reflect on the practice you have observed using a model of reflection. You can draw on the observee's reflections to further evidence your judgement of their practice. If you use the same model of reflection, this can enhance your discussions with specific pointers in the feedback session - comparing thoughts against the layers of the onion is often very illuminating.

One thing that you need to be specifically aware of is that Korthagen's onion model does not specifically mention power. We like to visualise a knife cutting through the onion and this is the 'power' - so that power is considered in relation to each layer of the onion. For example what did the environment 'say' in terms of power? (seating arrangements etc).

VACS Criteria

The VACS criteria has a long established basis in the assessment of professional practice. It involves the assessor considering any evidence they have gathered in relation to four key points:

Validity: This really involves questionning whether evidence is valid against the standard it is being presented for. In terms of direct observations, it is about considering whether the standards the observee hoped would be evidenced have been achieved. It also involves considering whether direct observation is a valid evidence method for the particular standard. For example, if a student claims that an observation provides evidence of their recording skills, direct observation won't be a valid assessment method unless the practice educator has also seen the recording which the student made of the piece of practice that was observed.

How?

Authenticity: Authenticity refers to whether the evidence is actually the person's own work (is it authentic?) This should be straightforward within the context of a direct observation. Although observers should be aware of the impact of another practitioner's behaviour and performance during an observation - remaining mindful of the influence this could have on their judgement of the observee's performance.

Consistency: This is about questionning whether there is evidence that practice is consistently at the required standard. For example, a practice educator working with a student should be satisfied that the observations carried out over the course of a student's placement demonstrate that they consistently practice in that way.

Sufficiency: Where evidence is going to be drawn from an observation, it is important to ensure that there is sufficient evidence to draw conclusions. For example, the observation might be of a meeting involving a number of people - unless the observee contributed significantly there may not be sufficient evidence of the observee's own practice on which to base conclusions.

Common sources of error

Drawing conclusions from direct observations is always a challenge. As we have covered, there is a level of subjectivity to any assessment of practice and making judgements is by no means an exact science. Using the VACS criteria and structuring your reflection using a specific model of reflection will help in making judgements, but it is also important to be aware that errors can occur in judging the evidence generated and drawing conclusions about direct observations of practice. The most common errors include:

First Impressions

The observer might draw conclusions based on the early part of the observation rather than keeping an open mind throughout the event being observed. It is particularly important not to do this because this is the stage when the observee is likely to be the most effected by their 'nerves'. Keep an open outlook throughout the event being observed.

How?

The halo / horns effect

The halo effect involves observers inferring good practice on the basis that the observee has previously demonstrated good practice. In the direct observation their practice might not be so good but the observer has inferred that the observee's practice will always be good. The horns effect is similar - but just the opposite. Based on previous poor performance, the observer expects the observee's practice to be poor.

Similar to me

This involves judging an observee favourably on the basis that they have carried out a piece of work like you would, or conversely, judging someone negatively but they have done something differently to you. It is important to remember that there are many different ways of carrying out a task. Just because someone does something in a different way to you doesn't mean they are not competent.

Inferring or Generalising

Don't work on the basis that because a practitioner can do A they must be able to do B, C and D. You can only draw conclusions based on what you have seen in the direct observation of practice.

How?

Contrast Effects

This arises when one person's performance is compared to another's by an observer. The inferior performance may then be deemed as not competent no matter how it stands against the criteria they are being assessed against. This is an error which is often seen in teams where one worker's performance is compared to another. It is important to remember that judgements should only be made in relation to requirements not in comparison with others.

Selecting the observation

Selecting the practice to be observed can throw up a range of issues. Wherever possible the observee should be encouraged to select the practice to be observed as this works towards addressing some of the power dynamics. However, where the observation of practice is a requirement for the assessment of a qualification, then the observer will want to have some input into the choice of observation. Where the observee choses the practice themselves, it is important to recognise that they are likely to select a piece of practice which they feel they are particularly skilled at or where they feel they have a good relationship with the service user. This might limit their opportunity to further develop their practice or to receive support with challenges. It is therefore vital to be clear with observees about the purpose of direct observations and the learning opportunities they can provide and to work collaboratively in selecting the practice to be observed.

How?

Providing Feedback

Tsui (2005) asserts that giving feedback to practitioners is an art. It is certainly true that it requires skill to provide effective feedback which enables people to learn from their experience. Feedback after an observation should come in two parts:

Informal feedback

Formal feedback

Informal Feedback

The timing of feedback following an observation is important as the observee will be keen to receive some immediate feedback on their practice. Whenever possible, it is good practice to provide some basic feedback as soon as the observation has ended. This could be provided in the car or back at the office immediately after the event. The feedback provided at this time will be limited and based on the observer's general feeling about how the observation went. It should also include an opportunity for the person who has been observed to express their own immediate reflections - including their views and feelings as to the outcome. Where the observation is contributing to some form of assessment, the person who has been observed is likely to seek reassurance that the observation went well or put bluntly "have I passed?" Either way, the observer must be honest that this feedback is immediate and informal - explaining that there will be an opportunity for a more comprehensive discussion at a later (specified) time.

How?

Formal Feedback

It is essential that any observation of practice is followed by the provision of formal feedback. Perhaps because of time restrictions, there can be a temptation to skip formal feedback, especially where an observation has gone well. However, this will limit the positive impact and minimise the benefits of direct observations.

Best practice is to plan a formal feedback discussion to take place a few days after the direct observation. If the direct observation forms part of a formal assessment, then it is likely that formal feedback needs to be recorded - probably in a set format.

Constructive Feedback

All feedback - whether it is formal or informal - must be provided in a constructive way.

It is the way that feedback is given, not the content of it that makes it constructive. Constructive feedback can be both positive (that is, reinforcing good practice) or negative (perhaps highlighting poor practice).

Constructive feedback provides information about knowledge and performance in such a way that the person receiving it maintains a positive attitude towards themselves, their practice, their work and the person giving the feedback. It encourages people to commit themselves to a personal action plan to move towards agreed standards of practice.

**IT'S NOT WHAT YOU SAY,
IT'S THE WAY THAT YOU
SAY IT!**

How?

Constructive Feedback	Destructive Feedback
Solves problems	Intensifies problems
Concentrates on behaviour / work performance	Concentrates on personality
Strengthens relationships	Damages relationships
Builds trust	Destroys trust
Is a two-way process	Is one-way
Reduces stress and tension	Adds to stress and increases tension
Manages conflict	Creates conflict
Helps development	Hinders development
Is assertive	Is aggressive
IS USEFUL	**IS USELESS**

The positive sandwich technique

Feedback should always start and end with
a positive. This approach is often referred
to as the 'positive sandwich'. The content or
'filling' of the sandwich is the area identified
for development - aspects of the observation,
that have been highlighted as needing more
work or improvement. The 'bread' of the
sandwich, being the positive aspects.

The concept is based on the notion that individuals will learn more when
feeling positive about themselves and their performance, building self esteem
and confidence. By starting with a negative the observer potentially negates
any constructive feedback that may follow. This also works on the principle of
an 'emotional bank balance', whereby withdrawals (negative feedback) cannot
be sustained without credit (positive feedback) being in place already.

How?

King (1999) refers to the need to focus on the crucial balance of support and challenge of feedback which does not allow either party to underplay strengths or address areas for improvement. The following framework is adapted from her work on how to maintain this balance.

 the observee is asked to start by identifying his or her own strengths

 the observer reinforces these and adds further strengths

 the observee is asked to identify areas for improvement

 the observer reinforces these, adding further areas if necessary

People are motivated when feedback is:

'Sandwiched' positively

Descriptive - of behaviour rather than the personality

Specific – rather than general

Sensitive - to the needs of the receiver as well as the giver

How?

Directed - towards behaviour that can be changed (for example, "You're too tall" is not helpful feedback!)

Timely - given as close to the event as possible (taking account of the person's readiness for feedback)

Selective - addressing one or two key issues rather than too many at once

Clear - avoid jargon wherever possible and check that the person receiving the feedback understands it

When feedback is difficult

Giving feedback can be difficult for a range of reasons. The person receiving the feedback may not always agree with it which may illicit an angry or tearful response. Although this is challenging for the person providing the feedback, it is important not to put off the feedback session. It can be that the person uses tears or anger in order to avoid the feedback.

What do I do if the person disagrees with the feedback?

If the recipient disagrees with the facts you are basing your feedback on then:

- give detailed examples
- check the areas of disagreement eg: "Do you think 'it' didn't take place or are you disagreeing about details of 'it'?"
- clarify the recipient's version of events and have an open mind

How?

If the recipient disagrees that a problem exists ("everyone makes mistakes") then explain the consequences of the action. Point out that making mistakes can constitute poor practice and that this needs to be addressed.

What do I do if they start crying?

If you ensure that your feedback follows the guidelines given, this is unlikely. However, if a recipient does cry when you are giving them feedback, then:

- be empathic eg: "I understand you will be shocked if no one has talked to you about this before"
- give permission for the person to cry (it can relieve stress)
- talk about why the recipient is finding the feedback upsetting
- try not to put off the session. It may be tempting to do so, but if you do, you will be leaving the recipient with the distress. Try to move on instead to finding solutions which will end the session on a positive note

What do I do if they get angry?

A natural defence mechanism when a person feels under pressure is anger. If a recipient becomes angry, then:

- ask the person why they feel (or appear to be) angry. They may not recognise that this is showing in their response
- ask the person if they would like to take a short break, but reconvene as soon as possible. Don't put off the feedback altogether, as you will be leaving the person with their anger. Instead, try to move on to look towards solutions
- be empathic eg: "I understand why you feel shocked/angry…."
- find something to say that reflects the recipient's circumstances eg: "I know that you are working hard on this area in difficult circumstances…."

How?

Recording the observation

The process by which observations should be recorded is not an exact science and each individual will have their own preferred style. However, it is important to reflect on the best method of how to record what is being observed. There is basically a continuum of options in terms of recording, ranging from recording everything to watching everything and recording nothing:

Record everything

Record nothing

Record everything!

One style is to record everything that occurs during the observation. Writing down every aspect of the process from what is being said to how it is being said is a comprehensive approach which provides the observer with a detailed record of the event. Patnaik and Becker (2012) state that the observer should *"record even the obvious or the seemingly unimportant"*. However, this tends to reduce the ability of the observer to be

sensitive to the dynamic of the interaction and may result in vital non verbal signs being missed. The observer may spend time all their time writing rather than observing.

How?

Watch everything!

At the other end of the spectrum is an argument for adopting a purely observing role. This involves simply "watching" the event and trying to engage with some of the less obvious dynamics between the participants without the distraction of having to record what is being observed. Foot Whyte (1984) asserts that it is important to recognise that a great deal of what is important to observe is unspoken. The approach of watching everything is really only effective if the observer is able to record in detail immediately after the observation has ended. There are some potential limitations with this approach, mainly because it is dependent on the reliability of the observer's memory. However, it is an approach that may prove effective in providing a more comprehensive assessment of an individual's performance, as it relies on the observer's core skills of listening, empathising and reflecting on the event being observed.

Combine the two: watch and record

Kemp (2001) discusses the recording of "sufficient key words or phrases" to highlight significant events in the observation that will enable the observer to later re-construct the observation and link the findings to the assessment criteria. Where the observer is clear about what formal recording will be required as a result of the direct observation (for example, if a direct observation report is required for a qualification), then this can help inform what key issues will be recorded. Recording specific elements of the observation against particular categories or agreed standards can also provide focus to the recording, while still enabling the observer to address the more subtle elements of the event. As Sanger (1996) states *"summaries of what has been said and what has not been spoken aloud"* taken together provide a *"holistic representation"* of the event.

How?

Direct Observation Reports

Where a direct observation is being carried out as part of the requirements for a qualification, there is likely to be a report pro forma. Often, the pro formas follow the process that we have outlined so that:

- the observee writes about their plans, objectives etc. prior to the observation
- the observee reflects on their thoughts following the observation
- the observer reports on what they saw and what evidence of practice was generated

If you are carrying out an observation for the purposes of a qualification, it is essential that you familiarise yourself with the report prior to the observation. Your knowledge of the report requirements will inform your recording during the observation.

Increasing Validity

Whilst direct observations of practice have a high face validity in terms of generating evidence of capability there are steps which can be taken to increase their validity further still. These steps include:

 Clarifying the objectives for assessment before the observation takes place. In this way the observer is clear about what they are looking for and can reflect on the evidence generated in a more systematic way.

 Triangulating the evidence generated. Triangulation is a method drawn from research. It can be used in relation to direct observations in two main ways, as covered on the following pages.

 Involving others in the process. This can negate the inherent difficulties related to the potential subjectivity of direct observations and again can take place in a range of ways as covered on pages 98 and 99.

How?

Triangulation

Triangulation is a concept drawn from research methodology. It is also useful to draw on in considering what evidence is needed when carrying out social work assessments.

Triangulation is based on the idea that there are three main sources of evidence (or assessment methods) as follows:

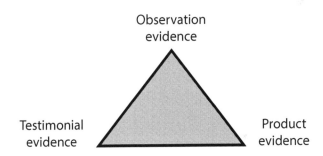

Observation
evidence

Testimonial
evidence

Product
evidence

In considering direct observations of practice, triangulation is useful in two main ways:

Recognising the importance of direct observation
Triangulation shows that direct observation is at the 'top' of the triangle in assessment methodology. This is essentially because it is such a reliable source of evidence with strong validity.

Triangulating observation evidence
To further ensure the validity of evidence generated from direct observations, the evidence can be 'triangulated'.

How?

Triangulating observation evidence

Triangulating observation evidence involves considering what you have 'seen' in the practice being observed, then exploring how this evidence can be further supported through:

Testimonial evidence: seeking feedback from the service user and anyone else involved in the practice being observed. It may also be appropriate to seek feedback on a wider basis from others who may be familiar with the work the practitioner is engaged in with that particular service user.

Product evidence: there will be some 'product' coming out of the practice that has been observed - usually the record that the practitioner completes (case notes, assessment forms etc). The observer could review this documentation to add further strength to the evidence generated.

Research mindedness

The assessment process which we have been exploring, dominates in terms of understanding direct observations of practice and is particularly useful in considering the stages of observations. However, following the assessment process in a procedural way can lead to mechanistic practice. It can be useful to use the research process to structure practice in observations. This is similar to the competence based assessment process although it is generally considered to be more dynamic.

PLANNING

GATHERING DATA

REPORTING RESULTS

ASSESSMENT PROCESS

How?

Adopting a researcher's mindset in relation to direct observation makes a lot of sense in that:

- direct observation has its roots in research methodology
- the observer is effectively researching the quality of the observee's practice - which involves not simply finding out what the practitioner does, but how they do it and why they do it in that way
- triangulation and observation are closely linked and triangulation is commonly used in research practice

Using a research mindedness approach to direct observations of practice means working in partnership with the observee to:

- select the practice event to be observed
- clarify the specific objectives for the observation

This means that the data required can be effectively generated and analysed.

Holistic assessment

The significant focus on competence based assessment in social work training in recent years has led to a criticism that social workers are being mechanistically assessed. For example, some students and practice educators appear to have taken a tick box approach to practice learning, reducing social work practice to a series of competencies to be ticked off.

Holistic assessment recognises that social work is both diverse and complex and therefore requires a richly textured approach to assessment.

To explain holistic assessment, the College of Social Work (2012) provides an analogy of eating a meal:

How?

"A holistic assessment is made when the meal is judged on its overall taste, quality and presentation etc. However, if one part of the preparation or an ingredient is missing or below standard, then this will impair the quality of the final product."

Developing this analogy can be helpful in understanding how to avoid mechanistic assessment in direct observations of practice. Think of the direct observation as eating a meal. What is it like? How has the observee prepared? Are they making use of the right ingredients? (their knowledge and skills). Is the recipe a good one? (what theory and approach are they using etc?)

Working in this way, rather than 'ticking off' specific tasks or skills will enable you to make a much more rounded assessment of the event being observed.

Involving others in direct observations

Where direct observations are being undertaken as part of a qualification programme, it is particularly useful for the assessor to involve others in carrying out direct observations of practice. Of course the assessor will want to observe some of the candidate's practice themselves, but to ensure that their assessment is valid and robust they should ask other practitioners to observe the candidate too. This can provide an important safeguard against subjective assessments and can offer the assessor a valuable 'second opinion'.

Many social work students now experience off site placement arrangements - which means they work with both an on site supervisor and an off site practice educator. In these circumstances, most programmes arrange for one of the observations to be carried out by the on site supervisor.

How?

In their guidance on holistic assessment, the College of Social Work (2012) suggest that trustworthy judgements involve observations of 'several slices of practice' carried out by 'different observers'.

Others will often be involved in carrying out informal observations of practice, but formalising these observations can be particularly useful in adding texture and depth to any assessment of a practitioner's capability.

It is important to ensure where others are asked to carry out direct observations of practice, they are clear on the requirements and employ best practice in observations.

Remaining person-centred in observations

Whilst everyone working in social work seeks to ensure their practice is person-centred, at times if people are focussing specifically on qualification requirements or particular procedures, the service user focus can be lost. It is essential to recognise that a service user's needs are always paramount and the needs of the observer and observee should never come before those of the service user. Never feel 'pushed' into practice which creates ethical concerns in relation to direct observations. It is not that long ago that NVQ assessors regularly observed direct care staff undertaking sensitive personal care tasks. Whilst understanding that direct observation is important in assessing a worker's capability, it is important to recognise how this infringes basic rights to dignity in care provision. However, it is easy to see how people can feel pushed into inappropriate practice to meet qualification requirements. Always remember that assessments of workers should not infringe the rights of service users and don't lose sight of user-centred practice.

How?

The hierarchy of observation

When considering the power dynamics inherent in direct observations, some practitioners focus exclusively on the power imbalance between observer and observee forgetting the issues of power for the service user. Tanner and Le Riche (1995) refer to the complex hierarchy in direct observations of students in placement. Service users are observed by the student who in turn is observed by the practice educator. The feelings of the service user and how they may view their position in this hierarchy must be addressed.

Roles within the observation process

The observer can fulfil various roles within the process. For example as Tanner (1998) highlights the observer may have the status of the 'expert', 'learner' 'professional' or 'assessor'. These roles will be interchangeable during the process, with the observer occasionally adopting more than one role at the same time. For example in order to assess, the observer must first learn to interpret the event taking place in front of them.

The expert role can be problematic as the flow of the observation may be interrupted by the service user or carer asking the 'expert' for their input. This can have the effect of undermining the observee's confidence as well as impacting on the remainder of the observation as the observer is perceived as leading the interaction therefore diminishing the influence of the observee's own practice.

How?

The professional role may have a similar impact as it is possible that the service user may view the role of the observee as secondary and may defer to the observer on the grounds that they are the 'professional'.

The various roles will also be interchangeable between participants. For example a student may adopt the role of learner as well as assessor. They may also be seen by the service user as the 'expert' or 'professional'. The service user may also be seen as the 'expert' as they are 'expert' in terms of their own experiences and feelings.

Which hat shall I wear?

The adopting of each of these roles highlights the potential impact of power dynamics and how this can manifest itself within the observation process. The observer needs to be able reflect on the impact of their role within the process and how to manage their 'power' appropriately.

Practical strategies to reduce the power imbalance

Encourage the observee to identify an appropriate event to be observed and highlight which standards they expect to meet in the observation

In preparation for an observation encourage the observee to set their own goals and objectives rather than just focus on the expectations of the observer

Encourage the observee to lead the de-briefing after the observation. The observee should reflect on their own objectives and whether they have been met effectively

Encourage the observee to identify their future learning goals following the observation

How?

Recognise the expertise of the service user and ensure that you don't simply pay 'lip service' to seeking user feedback

Maintain a person-centred approach at all stages of the observation process

Recognise, rather than deny, the power you have

Reflect on aspects of diversity at all stages of the observation

When to intervene

The presence of the observer in any observation will impact on the event being observed as the Hawthorne effect illustrates (see page 26). Considering the impact of the observer and when, and indeed if, they intervene is an important element to an effective observation.

> ...the researcher cannot exempt himself and ignores at his peril his own contribution to the social context of the experiment...
> (Argyris and Schön 1991)

When and if the observer should intervene will be different depending on the event being observed. However, the safety of the service user should be paramount in thinking about whether intervention should take place. For example, when adult or child protection issues are raised but not addressed by the observee or when information is shared or an action suggests that someone is at immediate risk it then may be appropriate for the observer to intervene.

How?

There will be occasions when the observee is struggling to manage the event effectively. They may provide inaccurate information, lose control of a meeting or 'dry up'. In these instances the observer will have to use their own judgement as to whether they intervene. This judgement will be based on the observer's knowledge of the observee and the potential impact on both the practitioner being observed and the service user.

The observation may involve expressions of emotion and distress which can encourage a response from the observer, however by responding to this show of emotion the observer can potentially short circuit the process and limit a real understanding of the event (Briggs 1992).

Allowing an observee to make their own mistakes can provide a fruitful learning opportunity for them and on balance it is often better to let the event run its course and address any issues afterwards.

If the observation has highlighted obvious discrepancies, then of course the observer will need to discuss these with the service user after the event to ensure that the observation has not been detrimental to their welfare.

Typology of participation and intervention (Humphrey 2007)

There is a clear difference between intervention and participation. Humphrey (2007) highlights this distinction and states that the observer can participate "subconsciously by making gesturing and utterances" but intervene deliberately by "seeking to alter a situation that is going awry".

Humprey developed a typology of participation and intervention in relation to the observation of social work students. The typology illustrates the way that evidence from direct observation can be 'contaminated' when observers *'stray into the realms of participation and intervention'.*

Humphrey's typology highlights the differences in the way that observers may intervene and illustrates that each individual assessor will have a preferred role in the process. The first position in Humphreys typology is that of the

How?

observer who is uncomfortable within their role of observer and 'retreats to frenzied note taking' which compromises their ability to observe. At the other end of the scale is the role of 'co-worker' in which the observer never allows the student to be observed in individual practice. This addresses some of the power issues inherent in the observation and assessment process but does not provide the opportunity for the student to demonstrate their competence as a solo practitioner.

There needs to be as much clarity as possible prior to the observation, about how the individual observer views their particular style and in what situations they would intervene and participate.

Humphrey's typology is particularly useful in recognising that 'intervention' doesn't simply mean stepping in – an observer could be intervening simply by nodding and making utterances. Understanding this can help observers reflect on the impact of their presence in the observation.

Service user feedback and involvement

Feedback from service users and carers is vital in relation to all aspects of social work practice and continual professional development. The majority of social work education and training programmes recognise this and make evidence drawn from such feedback a key part of programme requirements. Whilst feedback from service users will be occurring all of the time, it is common for this to be formally collected as part of the observation process. Very often observers will stay after the observation has ended and seek feedback from the service user at this stage. The way that this stage of the observation will be handled should form part of the preparation and planning for the observation, so that everyone knows how this will happen.

Ensuring that the service user has a choice about whether or not to provide feedback and how they want to provide feedback is the most important issue to consider.

How?

The feedback can be 'free flowing' and unstructured or may be structured by the observer asking questions. We tend to find a combination of the two provides the best quality feedback.

Structured questions

When asking questions of the service user, these can focus specifically on the observation experience, such as:

- Were you clear about what to expect today?
- What went well during the observation?
- What could have gone better?
- Did you get what you wanted out of the observation?

Or the questions can focus on the service user's wider experiences of work with the practitioner. For example:

- Do you find the worker reliable?
- Do you feel they are respectful of you?

- What do you think of the worker's communication?
- Does the worker carry out actions as planned? Can you give me some examples?

Use of scaling questions

We find scaling questions particularly useful in gaining feedback from service users and carers. For example - "on a scale of 1 to 5, how effective was the worker's communication?" It is really useful to follow such questions up with a more open question - so if the service user's response is 3 ask "what would they need to do to move the score up to a 5?" This can help provide clear feedback for the observee to help them to structure their future development.

Focussing on process rather than outcomes

When gathering evidence about the worker's practice, it is important to focus on the actual practice and the process the service user has experienced, rather than the outcome. A service user who is happy with the outcome of

How?

an assessment for example, may be very positive about the worker, whereas if someone is unhappy with the outcome of an assessment they might provide negative feedback - in both scenarios the feedback might not actually reflect the quality of the worker's practice. Focussing on specifics when seeking feedback encourages the service user to provide a more objective view of the practitioner's performance, rather than one based purely on outcomes.

Very often observees are particularly anxious about service user feedback following observations and are keen to hear the feedback. The feedback is therefore often shared during the informal feedback discussion (generally immediately after the observation). To make the feedback useful to the practitioner and to ensure that it doesn't become tokenistic, it is important to ensure that it is also discussed in the formal planned feedback session. We find asking the practitioner to reflect on the service user feedback, through asking the following questions, can be useful at this stage:

- What difference do you think being involved in providing feedback made to the service user?

- What surprised you about the feedback?
- How do you feel about the feedback?
- How might these feelings impact on your practice?
- What might you do differently as a result of the feedback?

The involvement of service users in the process of direct observation is part of a wider agenda to involve service users in social work education. As Kemp (2001) states *"service users cannot become participants in the assessment of students if they are powerless to influence the process."* The challenge for the observer is to avoid the possibility of service user feedback being tokenistic. For example, it can be useful to share the observation report with the service user and ask for their comments and feedback. The service user is after all an integral part of the event being observed, and it often occurs in their own home. They may want to make specific comments on the report of the observation. Clearly this should be discussed and agreed with the practitioner being observed - particularly as it is not currently standard practice.

How?

Challenges in user feedback

Whilst obtaining service user and carer feedback is vital, there can be significant challenges which the observer and observee need to consider and negotiate together:

- obtaining feedback immediately after the observation may be problematic because sometimes service users have simply 'had enough' at this point and just want everyone to leave. They may also want time to reflect and to see if the practitioner follows up as they have said they would. So would it be better to arrange a separate appointment to obtain feedback?
- service users may focus on the outcomes of the visit rather than on the practitioner's practice, as we have explored. How can you ensure the feedback remains balanced to ensure the process and practice is covered as well as the outcomes?
- the feedback may well be important to others, for example, if the feedback provides insights into systems and outcomes. How can the observer and observee ensure that this feedback is passed on as relevant?

Since service user feedback is often sought at the end of a direct observation of practice, it can be seen as an 'add on' - the icing on top of the cake. However, obtaining a service user's views is more than just the decoration on the cake, it is an integral part of the process which should be given sufficient thought.

Service user feedback isn't simply the icing on the cake. It's an integral part of making the cake!

How?

I really enjoy being involved, it made such a difference to me as it has built upon my confidence. People do listen to me and I can put my views across. It also improved my sense of self worth.

Having an impact as a service user or carer early on in someone's career is a crucial foundation for social work. It's important for trainee social workers to hear what has worked well and what has been unhelpful. There needs to be people out there who will listen to carers and see them as part of the solution, not part of the problem.

Comments from service user and carer in Elliot et al (2005)

Direct observation as a learning method

The major focus around direct observations tends to be on the use of observation as an assessment method. However, it is vital to recognise that direct observations also provide an important and valuable learning opportunity. Most adult learning theory highlights the importance of learning from experience. For example, andragogy (Knowles 1984) stresses the importance of experience providing the basis for self directed learning.

The law of exercise developed by Edward Thorndike works on the basis that adults learn best by taking part in an activity, and that to learn effectively an adult must take part in an activity in an environment where it usually occurs.

This focus on experience as a key prompt for learning is the basis for much of the work of Kolb (eg: 1984). Kolb stated that individuals need to go through a four stage cycle in order to learn. This learning cycle starts with a concrete experience which is seen as the focal point of learning, giving life, texture, and subjective personal meaning to abstract concepts.

How?

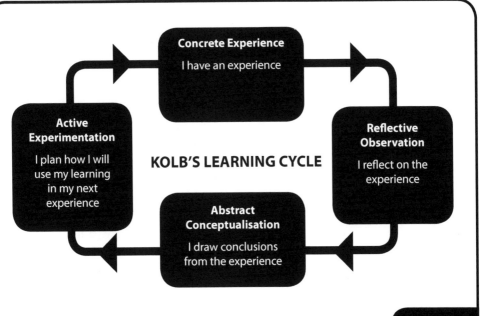

Concrete Experience

I have an experience

Active Experimentation

I plan how I will use my learning in my next experience

KOLB'S LEARNING CYCLE

Reflective Observation

I reflect on the experience

Abstract Conceptualisation

I draw conclusions from the experience

119

In many ways it is clear how direct observations of social work practice relate to Kolb's learning cycle - in that the event being observed is a concrete experience which can be learnt from. However, skilled facilitators of learning will recognise that observations of practice can actually provide an 'enhanced experience' in that it is not just the event that can provide a focus for learning. The planning for the observation and the feedback discussions after the observation provide additional concrete experiences to be learnt from.

Kolb's learning cycle illustrates how important it is to enable the learner to identify what they have learnt from the experience, draw conclusions and develop a plan of action to implement in their future practice. Understanding this process and using it to support the observee to move round the whole cycle of learning is particularly useful for observers.

It is useful to employ a coaching conversation to ensure that the observee moves fully around the learning cycle to maximise their learning, as follows:

How?

To assist the observee to move from the experience to **'reflective observation'** ask questions like:

- what do you think was happening there?
- how did you feel about that?

In supporting them to move into **'abstract conceptualisation',** ask questions that help them to make wider links and draw conclusions, such as:

- how does that link with theory / law? etc.
- what conclusions can you draw from that?

Finally, in supporting the candidate to move through the **'active experimentation'** stage, ask questions such as:

- what might you do differently next time?
- how will you put that into practice?

Reflective Practice and observations

Schön's work on reflection (eg: 1983) is well known in social work. Schön highlighted two key 'stages' of reflection:

| Reflection in action | Reflecting as an event is occurring |

| Reflection on action | Reflecting after an event has occurred |

Later, Killian and Todnem (1991) added a third stage of reflection:

| Reflection for action | Reflecting in preparation for an event |

How?

Effectively, this creates a reflection cycle:

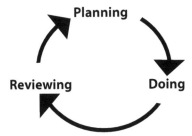

In order to promote effective reflective practice and good practice in direct observations, this reflective cycle demonstrates the importance of employing reflective practice techniques in:

- planning for the observation
- carrying out the observation
- debriefing and feeding back on the observation

Head, Heart, Tummy, Toes: a developing model for direct observation

One of the things we feel very strongly about is that practice wisdom should be much more valued in social work. Practitioners who are working in situations on a daily basis should be empowered to theorise on their practice and develop models for other practitioners.

Rachel Rayner is a practice educator who is a colleague of ours. As a practice educator, she is developing a model for direct observations based on a simple formula. Rachel works with children and wanted to ensure that her model was accessible to her service users which is reflected in its title. What follows is Rachel's explanation of her developing model.

How?

Social work is a relational model, one where we can use ourselves to connect, engage and build relationships with service users. If we don't know how we are feeling in situations, we may be at risk of losing valuable information about our own emotional state or that of the service user. Therefore, it is important that students learn to be emotionally aware. Our physiology informs our feelings and subsequent behaviour, but if we cannot make the links between what we are feeling, thinking and doing, we may not develop instinct or gut feelings that are a useful tool in social work. This simplistic model can be used by stakeholders to reflect on a direct observation and think about what went well, what could be improved, the "wow" moments and the times that made us uncomfortable. It is simplistic and visual as it helps make obvious the links students need to learn.

The planning before the observation will consider what the student and practice educator need to do to set the optimum environment for a "wow" moment, and prevent or mitigate against the toe-curling moments. The bits in-between are useful for developing good or even better practice.

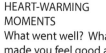

HAIR-RAISING MOMENTS
What were the moments that made you think "wow"? i.e. the things that shocked you; that you were not expecting? What gave you goose-bumps?

HEART-WARMING MOMENTS
What went well? What made you feel good about your work/practice? What are you proud of?

TUMMY-SINKING MOMENTS
What are the moments you think did not go as hoped? What, if anything, gave you the "sinking feeling"?
i.e. what might you do differently next time?

TOE-CURLING MOMENTS
What were the moments that made you feel uncomfortable? The moments that you had not/ could not plan for that you learn from the most?
i.e. the moments that in years to come you will look back and say, "I remember..."
These "awful" moments are often the ones that we learn from the most.

How?

The following pages contain some questions that can be used to enable the observer (in this model the practice educator), the observee (in this model the student) and the service user to reflect on the experience of the observation.

Question	Student	Practice Educator	Service User
Hair-raising moment ie: where something amazing happens, that is unexpected and surprising, all in a good way.	Were there any moments that shocked you? Anything that took you by surprise, that you had not expected?	Were there any moments that shocked you? Anything that had taken you by surprise, that you had not expected?	Were there any moments that shocked you? Did anything happen that took you by surprise, that you had not expected?

Question	Student	Practice Educator	Service User
Heart-warming moment ie: where you feel a sense of doing something competently	What were the moments that you thought went well? The practice that you feel was good, that you are proud of?	What were the moments that you thought went well? The practice that the student should feel proud of?	What do you think the student did well?

How?

Question	Student	Practice Educator	Service User
Tummy-Sinking moment ie: where you realise you could have done something differently for a better outcome.	What were the moments that you feel did not go as well? How did you recognise that they hadn't gone so well? What are the things you would change next time?	What were the moments that the student could have improved? What might the student need to change about their practice?	Were there any moments where you were not happy? Anything you would suggest the student do differently to improve their practice?

Question	Student	Practice Educator	Service User
Toe-Curling moment ie: made you feel uncomfortable	Was there anything that made you feel uncomfortable, that might have made you cringe, or your "toes-curl"? What have you learned from this observation?	Was there anything that made you feel uncomfortable in the observation? What learning is there for the student?	Was there anything that made you feel uncomfortable?

How?

Kolb (1984) believes that when human beings share an experience, they share it fully, concretely and abstractly. Whilst the observer, observee and service user will all share the experience, they will each experience it differently. Using a model such as that which Rachel is developing, which focusses on each person's understanding of specific aspects, can highlight differences as well as similarities in the experience, and can add validity to the observer's conclusions.

Using Technology

The use of technology such as a voice recorder or audio visual equipment for direct observation may be considered in certain scenarios but the use of such equipment is fraught with difficulties, such as:

- locating and using the necessary equipment can be problematic

- the use of such equipment is often more obtrusive than direct observation. As Jorgensen (1989) states *it is highly obtrusive in most situations*

- ethical and data protection issues are likely to reduce the extent to which technology could be used in an observation where members of the public are involved. Even if those issues were resolved, gaining the permission of the participants involved is likely to limit further the opportunities for the use of technology

How?

Technology is more likely to be used in situations such as a team meeting where only professionals would be attending. In these situations however, thought would need to be given as to what benefit recording the observation in this way would bring, whether it would provide any further clarity to the observation and whether it would be viewed unnecessarily obtrusive.

The use of technology might detract from the observation

It's not Rocket Science!

Direct observations of social work practice challenge both observers and observees. It is important to remember though that direct observation is not an exact science, and it's certainly not rocket science!

Good practice in direct observation is about:

- effective planning
- remaining service user focussed
- recognising the value of observations of practice
- providing constructive feedback
- being reflective, systematic and mindful about practice

How?

References

Argyris, C. and Schön, D.A. (1991) *Participatory Action research and action science compared: a commentary.* In W. Foot Whyte (Ed) Participatory Action Research. (California) Sage Publications.

Atherton, J. S. (2011) *Teaching and Learning: Assessment - direct observation.* Available online at: www.learningandteaching-info/teaching/assessment-direct.htm. Accessed 3.3.12.

Bernard, H. R. (2006) *Research Methods in Anthropology: Qualitative and Quantitative Approaches.* (4th edition) (Oxford) AltaMira Press.

Berra, Y. (2008) *You Can Observe A Lot By Watching: What I've learned about teamwork from the Yankees and life.* (New Jersey) John Wiley and Sons.

Branfield, F. (2007) *User involvement in social work education: Report of regional consultations with service users to develop a strategy to support the participation of service users in social work education.* (London) Social Care Institute for Excellence.

Briggs, S. (1992) *Child Observation and Social Work Training.* Journal of

Social Work Practice. 6(1) pp. 49-61. Available online at: www.bmj.com/content/318/7200/S2-7200.full. Accessed 12.4.12.

College of Social Work (2012) *Understanding what is meant by holistic assessment.* (London) College of Social Work.

Cowburn, M., Nelson, P. and Williams, J. (2000) *Assessment of Social Work students: standpoint and strong objectivity.* Social Work Education Vol 19(6) pp. 627-637.

Danbury, H. (1994) *Teaching Practical Social Work.* (Aldershot) Arena. Ashgate Publishing Ltd.

Foot Whyte, W. (1984) *Learning from the Field. A Guide from Experience.* (London)Sage Publications.

French, J. and Raven, B.H. (1959) *The bases of social power.* In Cartwright (ed) Studies in Social Power. pp. 150-167. (Ann Arbor) Institute for Social Research.

Hu, J. (2011) *Tools and Techniques: Direct observation.* Available online at: www.idemployee.id.tue.nl/g.w.m./UFTdirectobservation.pdf. Accessed 7.9.12.

How?

Humphrey, C. (2007) *Observing Students' Practice (Through the Looking Glass and Beyond)*. Social Work Education. 26(7) pp. 723-736.

Inner London Probation Service (1993) *Working with Difference: A positive and practical guide to anti-discriminatory practice teaching*. (London) ILPS.

Jorgensen, D. L. (1989) *Participant Observation. A Methodology for Human Studies*. (California) Sage Publications.

Kemp, E. (2001) *Observing Practice as participant observation - linking theory to practice*. Social Work Education 20 (5) pp. 527-538.

Kemshall, H. (1993) *Assessing Competence: Scientific Process or Subjective Inference? Do we Really See it?* Social Work Education 12(1) pp. 36-45.

Killian, J. and Todnem, G. (1991) *Reflective judgement concepts of justification and their relationship to age and education*. Journal of Applied Developmental Psychology, 2(2) pp. 89-116.

King, J. (1999) *Giving Feedback*. BMJ online. Available online at: www.bmj.com/content/318/7200/S2-7200. Accessed 20.3.13.

Kingston, P. and Smith, D. (1983) *Preparation for Live Consultation and Live Supervision when working without a one way screen.* Journal of Family Therapy 5(3) pp. 219-33.

Knowles, M. (1984) *Andragogy in Action.* (San Francisco) Jossey Bass.

Kolb, D. (1984) *Experiential Learning: Experience as the Source of Learning and Development.* (New Jersey) Prentice Hall.

Korthagen, F. (2005) *Practice, Theory and Person in Lifelong Professional Learning.* In Beijaard, D., Meijer, P., Morine-Dershimer, G. and Tillema, H. (Eds) Teacher Professional Development in Changing Conditions. (Netherlands) Springer.

Le Riche, P. (1998) *The Dimensions of Observation. Objective Reality or Subjective Interpretation.* In Le Riche, P. and Tanner, K. (Eds) Observation and its Application to Social Work. (London) Jessica Kingsley.

Le Riche, P. and Tanner, K. (1995) *You see but you do not observe. The Art of Observation and application to practice teaching.* Issues in Social Work Education 15(2) pp. 66-80.

How?

Le Riche, P. and Tanner, K. (1996) *The Way Forward: Developing an Equality Model of Observation for Social Work and Education*. Issues in Social Work Education 16(2) pp. 3-14.

Lloyd Webber, S. (2010) *Writing from Direct Observation*. Available online at http://stephenlloydwebber.com/writing-guides. Accessed 30.9.12.

Murell, J. (1993) *Judgement of Professional Competence: Bags of Bias*. In Preston-Shoot, M. (ed) Assessment of Competence in Social Work. (Bournemouth) Social Work Education, Special Publication pp. 5-19.

Patnaik, D. and Becker, R. (2012) *Direct Observation: Some Practical Advice*. Available online at www.jumpassociates.com/direct-observation-some-practical-advice.html. Accessed 28.9.12.

Perberdy, A. (1993) *Observing*. In Shakespeare, P., Atkinson, D. and French, S. Reflecting in Research Practice. Issues in Health and Social Welfare. (Buckingham) Open University Press.

Rothlisberger, F. J. and Dickson, W. J. (1939) *Management and the Worker*. (Cambridge) Harvard University Press.

Sanger, J. (1996) *The Compleat Observer? A Field Research Guide to Observation.* (London) Farmer Press.

Schön, D. (1983) *The Reflective Practitioner: How Professionals think in action.* (London) Temple Smith.

Skills for Care (2013) *Social Work: Informing judgements and processes.* Available online at www.skillsforcare.org.uk. Accessed 21.3.13.

Spielberger, C. D. (2004) *Encyclopedia of Applied Psychology: Volume 1.* (Oxford) Elsevier Academic Press.

Tanner, K. (1998) *Towards an Equality Model: Observation through a power lens.* In Le Riche, P and Tanner, K (Eds) Observation and Its Application to Social Work. (London) Jessica Kingsley.

Trowell, J. and Miles, G. (1991) *The contribution of observation training to professional development in social work.* Journal of Social Work Practice 5(1) pp. 51-60.

Tsui, M.S. (2005) *Social Work Supervision Contexts and Concepts*. (London)Sage Publications.

University of York (2000) *Facts, Feelings and Feedback: A Collaborative Model for Direct Observation*. (York) University of York.

Weade, G. and Evertson, C. M. (1991) *On what can be learned by observing teaching*. Theory into Practice 30 (1) pp. 37-45.

Williams, S. and Rutter, L. (2007) *Enabling and assessing work-based learning for social work: supporting the development of professional practice*. (Birmingham) Learn to Care.

Wilson, J. and Corlett, N. (2005) *Evaluation of Human Work*. (3rd Edition). (Florida) Taylor and Francis Group.